Science Enquiry

IS IT LIVING OR NON-LIVING?

Lisa M. Bolt Simons

raintree

a Capstone company — publishers for children

Raintree is an imprint of Capstone Global Library Limited, a company incorporated in England and Wales having its registered office at 264 Banbury Road, Oxford, OX2 7DY – Registered company number: 6695582

www.raintree.co.uk
myorders@raintree.co.uk

Edited by Erika L. Shores
Designed by Dina Her and Juliette Peters
Original illustrations © Capstone Global Library Limited 2022
Picture research by Eric Gohl and Kelly Garvin
Production by Tori Abraham
Originated by Capstone Global Library Ltd
Printed and bound in India

978 1 3982 2538 1 (hardback)
978 1 3982 2537 4 (paperback)

British Library Cataloguing in Publication Data
A full catalogue record for this book is available from the British Library.

Acknowledgements
We would like to thank the following for permission to reproduce photographs:
Getty Images/Samantha Mitchell/Corbis/VCG, 28; iStockphoto: FatCamera, 7, lmforthand, 29, MarcoAMazza, 19, ssj414, 5; Science Source/STEVE GSCHMEISSNER, 15; Shutterstock: Alex Tihonovs, 23, Arteck555, 11, Choksawatdikorn, 17, eva_blanco, 4, hans engbers, 1, 9, Ingus Kruklitis, 25, Iryna Kalamurza, 12, Jill Lang, 8, JRJfin, 21, Kenneth Sponsier, 22, Nuk2013, cover, Nurlan Mammadzada, 24, schankz, 27 (bottom), thka, 13, Vitaly Korovin, 27 (top), Zebra-Studio, 20.
Artistic elements: Shutterstock/balabolka.

CONTENTS

Words in **bold** are in the glossary.

INVESTIGATION: IS IT LIVING OR NON-LIVING?

Your family just got a new puppy! How do you look after it? You feed it. You give it water. Food and water will help the puppy grow. It may one day have its own puppies! A puppy is a living thing.

What if you have a pet rock? Will it eat food and drink water? Will it grow? Will it have baby rocks? If you said no, you're correct! Rocks are not living things.

Now let's do an **investigation**.
Get a piece of paper and a pencil.
Draw a line down the middle of the
paper. On one side write, "living".
On the other side write, "non-living".

Go outside and make **observations**.
Think about the puppy and the rock.
What needs water? What grows?
Draw pictures of three things you
think are living. Then label them with
their names. Draw pictures of three
things you think are non-living. Then
label them.

HOW DO WE KNOW WHAT IS LIVING?

At first you may think that what moves is a living thing. A puppy moves! It's a living thing! Water moves. But it is not a living thing. A car moves. But it is not a living thing.

There are also living things that don't move. Think about mushrooms and toadstools in a forest. Or think about coral deep in the sea. Living things have other **traits** besides movement. Let's learn about them!

Remember the puppy? The puppy is made of **cells**. Cells are the smallest parts of a living thing. You have cells too!

A puppy needs food and water. Scientists call food and water **nutrients**. These nutrients give the puppy energy. Nutrients also help the puppy grow. Being able to grow is a trait of a living thing. Non-living things do not grow. Remember the rock? The rock will never grow.

What are other traits of living things? If the puppy gets scared, it might run away. Or it might bark. It might even bite! The puppy is responding to its **environment**, or the world around it. Living things react to what is happening around them. The rock will never respond to anything around it. It will never be scared!

Finally, living things reproduce. To reproduce means to make more of the same kind.

WHICH THINGS ARE LIVING?

You can't see the smallest living things with your eyes. You need to look through a microscope! **Bacteria** are living things. A spoonful of lake water can have as many as 1 million bacteria cells. That's how small bacteria are! Each is made from a single cell. It moves. It eats. It also reproduces.

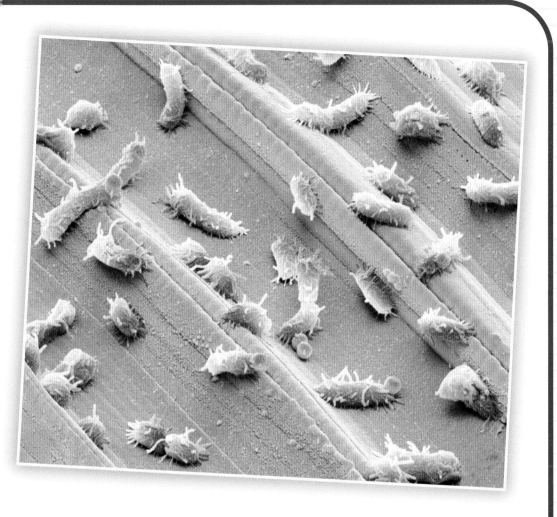

Some bacteria are good. They can help prepare food like cheese. Bacteria are also needed when making some medicines. Some bacteria are bad. They can cause illness, such as strep throat.

Protozoans are also living things. They have single cells like bacteria. But they are bigger. Sometimes you can see protozoans without a microscope. There are more than 50,000 **species** of protozoans! These living things have a life cycle. They eat. They reproduce.

Protozoans are found in every habitat. Some species are not harmful to animals. But some can be dangerous. They can cause animals, including humans, to get very ill.

Have you ever seen the sea? Did you see something that looks like long, green grass in the water? If so, it might have been kelp. Giant kelp can grow up to 50 metres (164 feet) long!

Giant kelp is a type of **chromist**. Chromists are living things. They grow. Most chromists use the sun to help them make food. They reproduce. Other chromists can't be seen without a microscope.

Do you like mushrooms on pizza?
If so, you eat **fungi**! Fungi is a living
thing. Fungi has many cells. It grows.
It eats. It reproduces.

Fungi is found on land. It's also found
in water and in the air. Fungi is even
found in animals and plants!

Some fungi is used to help make medicine. Other fungi called mould is not good. That's what you find growing on old cheese or old leftover food. Yuck!

Remember your walk outside? Did you see any plants? Plants are living things, of course! They have many cells. They grow. They use the sun to help make food. They reproduce.

There are almost 400,000 species of plants. Most of these grow flowers. Plants make **oxygen** for living things to breathe. People and animals eat plants. Plants can help make medicines.

Pigeons are common birds in big cities.

What else did you see outside? What could be the last group of living things? That's right! Animals! Humans are a type of animal. Animals have many cells. They grow. They eat and drink. They reproduce.

Remember the puppy? Animals respond to their environment. They can find a warm, sunny spot if they get cold. They can run away if a bigger animal comes too close.

A turtle sits in the sun to warm up its body.

What happens when a living thing dies? Scientists say it is a living thing that is dead. The living thing used to be alive.

A non-living thing, such as a pencil, a notebook or an eraser was never alive. This also means non-living things don't die.

Ask these questions to find out if something is living or non-living:

- Does it have cells?
- Does it need food and water?
- Does it grow?
- Does it respond to its environment?
- Does it reproduce?

HOW DO WE LOOK AFTER LIVING AND NON-LIVING THINGS?

People look after things differently. If a thing is living, it needs nutrients to grow. It's like the puppy. If it's non-living, it doesn't need food or water. It's like the rock.

We don't give shoes nutrients. But we still look after them. We keep shoes clean. We don't give a phone nutrients. But we still look after it. We try not to drop a phone.

The world is full of living and non-living things. What are all the living and non-living things you look after in your own life?

GLOSSARY

bacteria one celled, tiny living things; some are helpful and some cause disease

cell tiny structure that makes up all living things

chromist living thing that includes some algae and protozoans

fungi living things similar to a plant but without flowers, leaves or green colouring

investigation search for facts to solve a problem or answer a question

nutrient part of food that is used for growth

observation make note about what is seen or noticed

oxygen colourless gas that people and animals breathe in order to live

protozoan tiny living thing whose body is a single cell

species group of plants or animals that share common characteristics

trait characteristic or feature

FIND OUT MORE

BOOKS

Living Things (Science in a Flash), Georgia Amson-Bradshaw (Franklin Watts, 2018)

What Living Things Need series, Karen Aleo (Raintree, 2020)

WEBSITES

www.bbc.co.uk/bitesize/topics/z6882hv/articles/zs73r82
Learn how to tell what is living and non-living with this BBC Bitesize video.

www.dkfindout.com/uk/animals-and-nature/what-is-living-thing/
Find out more about living things with DKFindout!

INDEX